The Turning Key

Contents

For (Her)
From (Him)

Also
For Janet
Your encouragement and support during those times of
winter, when my work needed that extra edge and focus,
is a debt I can never repay.
Thank you.

"The Turning Key" includes poems that were previously
published. Some have been reimagined,
but their meaning has been retained.

Some poems were originally published in
"Nightingale and Dreaming"
"Swing Me Your Bones"
"Machine Whispers"
"Ghost in the Mirror"
"No Mayo"
Those titles are no longer available.

Others were taken from,
Neil's poetry ramblings (neilspoetry.blogspot.com)
Poetry not previously available in the above titles,
or elsewhere, are published in "The Turning Key"
for the first time.

Externally themed poems can be read at:
From One Line To Another (Kobayaashi Studios)
The Unseen (Kobayaashi Studios)
Lothlorien Poetry Journal (Lothlorien)
Unheimlich (Soyosbooks)
(Neil)

And as the chords of life's symphony,
gently rise and express their magic.
The stage is set for the encore of eternity.
Where the silence is ear shattering.

Tomorrow

Embark, whispered the seraph.
Together, we'll navigate the oceans' vast embrace.
Through the misty veils, we'll find firm shores.
Ascend into the woods.
Gaze past the sentinel trees
Let dawn's light gleam on our upturned faces.
Revel in the warmth of summer's brightness.
Watch the albatross's grand, soaring flight.
Such wonder is held in heaven's vault.
Yet, hold close the kinship's gentle balm.
In memories' glow, let hearts exalt.

Fishermen

And when twilight veils the horizon,
The fishermen return to shore.
Their weary bodies adrift in the salt-kissed air.
But eyes remain sharp, ever-searching.
for the flicker of silver fin beneath the surface,
the glimmer of hope that dances in the depths,
beckoning them to set sail once more.

Bound by the unwavering call of the sea,
forever drawn to the rhythm.
And so they cast each day anew.
for in each sunrise lies infinite possibility.
and in each wave, a chance at redemption.

In the evening's gentle embrace,
Eyes gaze at the heavens.
Weathered hands clasped in gratitude
For the bounty harvest brought forth.
With a heart overflowing, whispered,
"Thank you, dear sea, for your gifts bestowed,
For in this dance of fate we have
found our true home."

Travellers

Sunset's amber hues embrace the horizon.
Stars, like diamonds, adorn the sky.
Guiding weary souls through countless nights,
Under the watchful eye of the crescent moon.

Sinuous silhouettes dancing with the wind,
Tracing stories of love and loss in the sand.
Comments of secrets whispered in the darkness,
Carried away by the desert's voiceless breath.

Tales of trade and adventure rise with the morning
As weary travellers break their bread and rest.
A tapestry of cultures woven under the sun,
Bound by a shared thirst for life's delightful essence.

Heatwaves shimmer, reflecting mirages of hope.
As caravans traverse the vast expanse.
Weaving threads, connecting lives in fleeting moments,
In this transient oasis, dreams are born.

Breath Of Eve

Silent tendrils float in the air.
as delicate threads of silk,
weaving through the awakening earth,
softly caressing petals and dew-kissed leaves.
Eve's breath dances, weightless and ethereal.
stirring the slumbering tendrils of life.

It carries a blossoms' fragrance .
delicate and sweet,
the whispers of a lover's promise,
breathing secrets into the wind.
Ancient melodies of forgotten tales
are sung through the breath of Eve.

From the highest mountain top
to the deepest valley's embrace,
Her touch is carried on gentle streams.
bringing solace to weary hearts.

In her breath, hope is born anew.
restoring strength in a weary traveller.

The Devil's Waltz

In dim-lit halls where shadows dance, restraint dissolves.
The fiddler's bow draws sin, hunger, and haunting.
Each step and turn, a whispered pact, desire's resolve,
Temptation twirls its partner close.
Beneath cold eyes that stare in silence, smirk, and brawl,
The Devil grins, as mortals spin, 'til daylight calls.

And in this waltz, the soul is swayed and always lost.
Till dawn's light breaks, the music fades against hallowed
walls.Stellar dust in sombre night, Twilight's veil, consumer
upon the howling tempest
An elegy all shattered,
Where screaming angels pursue their prey.

In The Light

With dust and debris from Saturn's moons,
Casting shadows over the horizon.
Titan and Enceladus are perhaps playing games.
Maybe remember their beginning,
When God said, "Let there be light,"
"So I can take the universe for a spin."

Fireflies

In the depths of time a flickering light ignites.
Fireflies romance, casting their shimmering theatre
A waltz of nature with tiny lanterns
Ablaze in the darkness
Guiding souls through the silk rain
A cosmic ballet
That meanders through eternal meadows
Moonlit dreams.

The Midnight Air

I dream of clowns performing songs.
And twirling batons in perfect harmony.
Their painted faces are so merry and profound.

A symphony of laughter, a circus in tune.
Sounding gongs and jingles.
Balloons dancing, colours colliding, blending.

Bringing joy to the heart, banishing gloom.
With every note, with every castle.
Voices, seashells, whisper delight.

Each word emerges with a harmony of sound.
Lifting our spirits.

Holy Ground

By the shushing sea, we'll walk, watching breakers flee.Our
kiss is not of flesh but of a union of souls.Salvation's hour
approaches swiftly, and my courage shall not fold.

Aloft on ether wings, o'er vale and hill we'll glide,Such
wondrous love our hearts reveal—this truth we shall see.
Be still, my love, and hear my voice rise to a celestial sound.
I see thee wait, anticipation sown, on holy ground.

Sea Of Faces

But as I seek, my eyes meet unfamiliar faces.
With ancient glances, 'tis fear's peculiar.
A troupe of actors, playing on life's stage,

Their scripted roles presented,none escaped.
At times, I catch a glimpse of tears unshed.

Within their depths, fear and pain are widespread.
Yet 'neath their masquerade they soldier on,
For life demands an unyielding heart.
Anon.

Upon The Hill

Moon-bathed, she threaded warmth through the summer's
    breath.
As the heavens exhale, clouds pilgrimage to the dreams' cradle.
Angels, mystic titans, supped on her melody,
Chewing the rhapsody, jaws grind the twilight's hush.
Each note is a ripple, each cadence a softened claw on the
    ear's drum.
While Earth, the old priest, harrumphed Amen from under
    its leafy steeple.

Sandwich

In the mist of winter's silent embrace,
A solitary creation, disregarded and cold,
Each ingredient's colour becomes a whisper.
As ghosts cover its resting place.
Once golden, it is now pale and mute.
Embracing the remnants of flavours past,
A tableau of memories locked in frozen time.

Forever Yours

Above the wispy suns, I soar and seize.
Imbibe my soul with melodies.
In hearts replete,
We merge into the hues of twilight's vast expanse.

I murmur, playful as the breeze.
As the wayward cuckoo sows its mischief,
In the hollows, fledglings sing.

Elders reminisce, time-transfixed,
On chairs sun-bleached in threadbare tweed,
While youths exult in the purest tone,
Their laughter across the meadows was free.

Infinity in my clasp, refined,
My luminescence, though distant,
I am ever-present, woven into this private theatre.
Forever yours.

Mouse

With the hat atop its tiny head,
And the scarf draped 'round its neck,
The mouse looked rather dapper and said,
"Ready to face the wide world's speck."

Though small in stature and bold at heart,
Its spirit set the cold ablaze.
The mouse ventured out as art.
Into winter's sting, unfazed.

Through snow-covered fields, it danced.
It tirelessly strayed, embracing frost.
The chilly season romanced
With rhythm, not a note is lost.

And as the winter would whisper softly,
With lullabies that made night yawn,
The mouse trudged through the snow.
Enchanted, beauty's spell was drawn.

With every step, a tale spun wide.
It defied the cold's claim of demise.
A tiny warrior, cast aside,
Immune to the cold's fierce, icy cries.

Superhero

As their heads haunch backwards,
Dreaming towards the sky.
Beneath cloaks and mirrors,
Pretending to be a superhero.
Even the trees flex through the foliage mask.
Yet it is sensible to realise that once the game is up.
It's down to earth with a bump.
Normality shines.
Knowing forever that good deeds,
Always deserve the applause.

Flute

Graceful birds of ebony-flute.
Dancing in moonlit skies.
Their wings softly brush.
Against the chambers of my heart.
Whispering melodies were never sung.
By the tongues of mortal kinfolk.

Their words are a balm to my spirit.
Awakening dormant embers.
An enchanted fire deep within.
And as I close my eyes,
I can feel their tender embrace.
Lulling me to sleep.

With their dulcet lullabies.
They become the rhythm of my heartbeat.

A Feline Ghost

Whispers of velvet fur, beneath moon's hollow leer, yet shadows dance, claws fearsome.

A sinister serenade cloaked in night's ice, a spectre's tune, bending the will.

In the darkness' tight embrace, where silence dares to sing, the failed fiend's approach—so graceless—

Tangled in Twilight's web, where secrets dwell and thrive, the cat's guise sheds, eyes piercing.

Gleaming orbs afloat, unbound by earthly ties, their eerie glow—a truth that brags about cat naps.

Amidst the hushed and dreaming world, they hear the silent cries.

Emerging tales spun from the feline's cryptic guise, weaving through dreams—mysterious.

Sacred

Within the flowing lease,
Between dusk and mid-summer.
You and I, threading our timeline,
Saw nature at play.

On the windswept shore.
Below the painted sky.
Searching for treats from discarded waste,
By the fishermen of the fleet.

Whose skill on the sea,
Was born upon tears of their forebears.
As Gannet and Guillemot companions,
Rested upon salty sprayed air,

Near cliffs and sandy dunes.
Weathered by pen and paper.
Yet their pace and lingering,
Was unfettered by the constraints of this life.

As they bonded forever,
Flapping their wings,
Within heated squabbles.

Eyes Of The Night

The snow, gnashing its frosted teeth,
forced its way through the window sills.
Wolves breaching fragile confines.
Little mice, whisper-voiced survivors,
Glancing at their options with silent precision,
Each nibble a testament to their shrinking dominion.
Blinkered lights, lidless eyes of the night,
Pierced through the thick haze that veiled the moon,
A spectral orb, a ghostly watchman over a withering world.
A child in her ageless wisdom,
Parted the clouds with innocent curiosity,
Her breath a fragile bloom in the icy air.
Winter with her crystalline talons,
Draped her chilling coat over the land,
A silvered reckoning, sharpening the bones of earth,
Setting the stage for the ungodly ballet,
The season's run, a relentless pursuit,
Life locked in the raw,
Primaeval struggle.

Mate

I miss your company.
Your clumsy incantations over the charcoal cauldron of tea,
Mishaps are rising as betrayed hope.

The hollow bursts of laughter from your eyes, conspirator,
Howled echoes through an indifferent void.
I miss your groans, a daily dirge in the damp bathroom,
Entangled in the absence of bath-time shrouds.

I miss the chill of your feet beneath the covers.
Your grudging acceptance to conjure Dawn's cup.

I miss the broth, steam kissing the window panes,
Life is distilled in the cauldron of winter's breath.

Your rituals under the apple tree, a shaman of old gibberish,
Whirling thrice—something primitive charging the soil,
The ancient Greeks called the fruit to swell.
I miss your arrival, shadow swallowing the threshold,

My vigil by the flicker of oil,
Scorching time with worry—that you come back too late.
But most of all, I miss the gate's closing clang.
The soft missiles of your cheeky grin.

Secret Escape

Amidst the green and gold,
The rolling hills unfurl their curves and dips.
Soft breezes dance with daffodils and dills.
A sweet escape from life's tumultuous angst.
Their peaks and valleys,
A calm symphony of earth and sky.
And all that dwells between their gentle slopes,
A balm for eyes weary.
Their vast expanse is a surrealistic sea.
Where verdant meadows meet the horizon.
And tranquil streams weave a path.
A peaceful haven where the soul can fly.
To let go of all that it needs to withstand.

Second Dream

Dream of empty tins with pennies spent.
In human eyes, sight is priceless.
As hands grapple with the tin whistle,
To revolutionise the night.
Perhaps angel wings will flap in unison.

Tom's cat meows to the midnight choir.
Candles on the hill light up the way.
Change is nigh, amidst the world's great pyre.
The full moon shines lilac.
Magic fills the air with every breath.

With every step we take, we shape our fate.
And challenge fear, with nothing left to bet.
For what is life if not a grand design?
Of dreams, in hope,
And love's sweet Valentine.

Moonlight

As shadows dance in the midnight air,
Whispers hint at secrets,
While phantoms glide atop the moonlight.
With bated breath, we feel their haunting eyes.
Behold their spectral forms that flicker.
Shivering as their ghostly sighs wail,
To warn of dangers.
Their touch is made of frost.
Yet laughter echoes through the halls.
With songs of melodies.
These melancholy reminders,
Of endless mournings, sweet.

Schedule In Breakfast

Chaos sprawls on the breakfast table, weaving its tales.
Little babies pecking at the eyes of mothers.
Their mouths, gaping into the abyss of the dawn chorus,
Sounding the maelstrom of morning's primal song.

Father Time fumbles with his diary.
Post-ablution, his transformation from an ancient enigma
To a bewildered little boy lost in a labyrinth of clutter,
His work toys—a legion of mundane tasks—scattered, waiting.

Crunching numbers, jumbled visceral threads,
Tickling the dry skeletons of brains, starved of breath,
While keys clash in a metallic symphony,
Stirring the air as doorbells herald the exit.

Hero Shanks's pony, that stalwart steed of shoe leather,
Skips away, bearing the weight of pedestrian chaos,
Into the forest of forgotten drama.
The mundane epic of existence unfolds.

Pull The Plug

Prayer was the boss in this echo chamber.
A hurricane so sick with a heavy cold.
Aimless ships begged their captains for hope.
Bragging waves splashed salt everywhere.
And from their endeavours,
Touched the moon.
Fading light shared its influence with a shut eye.
Painted skies mocked the artist,
Clearly drunk,
After too many late-night performances.
Yet on went the wood and ply.
Now glued in pieces.
With mermaids yelling
Instructions to Neptune.
Pull the plug.
Or all shall be lost.

Epitaph

And all the while, poppies expose themselves.
To impress the fields.
Morning orchestral manoeuvres have begun.
Into the ears of the living.
While whispering love sonnets and reading their notes,
Fingers caressed wavy hair.
Their scarlet ribbons are flowing in the wind.
Ripples of applause from beneath silken gowns,
As flesh and bone,
Previously as cold as marble,
Awoke to dance.

Scarecrow

A motionless observer of changing skies, hands outstretched in supplication. Unheard crows perch upon weary shoulders, pecking at grains of forgotten dreams.

As autumn's breath weaves through his shroud.

A sentinel of seasons now past, eternal witness to nature's dance. Of the soil's embrace and the sun's golden touch.

In stillness, he yields to nature's course. Rooted as earth drinks the rain.

But when twilight cloaks the verdant land, the scarecrow whispers to the hidden moon, of wisdom gleaned from shadowed nights, of words unsaid, of hopes forgotten.

For in the heart of every scarecrow lies a kernel of our own essence. A symbol of resilience, birthed by love, whispers,"Fear not, my dear, for you are enough."

Phoenix

For now, it was the time of exploding ships as journeys'
    ends loomed near graveyards'.
In sleepy whispers, the cosmos hums eulogies as stars weep
    for the fallen.
Where light retreats to shadows, the vast unknown cradles
    history's tales.
A sky ballet of celestial demise echoes through the eternal isles.
Yet amidst the wreckage, a phoenix may yet rise,
    undeterred in the infinite expanse.
Life's persistence, a testament to time, is in this garden,
    untamed and grand.
Crafted from dust, its wings unfold, voyaging through the
    quiet, star-studded swirl.
Among the remnants, bold seeds of knowledge bloom,
    charting paths through the profound cosmic expanse.

Without Limits

With motley garb, they weave illusion's dance.
Boundless laughter, through Folly's lens,
Harlequins Unbound.
Cunning as cold as Santa on winter's eve.

A trick of light and heart, they dance on life's string.
They speak in riddles.
With bells that chime, their fate is reserved.
They pull from stony hearts, a victory unwritten.

Roll The Bones

Doing a jig as a skeleton
through the hollows in my socks
There are no nails in my soul.
Only wood clippings
And a smell of mystical desire
To flourish in faith
And excite my flames.
Of enthusiasm.

Upon The Slope

Winter's breath lingers on my tongue.
A sharp tang, as though the clouds themselves
imbibed by Earth's cold nectar.
Breezes whisper omens in chilled tones.
Heather embraces insinuating through the weave.

Leaking boots—a scarce barricade against the dawn.
My woollen hat—a stitched sentinel
against the fierce kiss of the wild.
Livestock huddle, a congregation beside the brook,
Murmuring waters barely perturbed beneath
the storm's wide, relentless meltdown.
Spectral mists descend, a ghostly
benediction.

Paper Moons

A million twinkling freckles,
Painted on a vast canvas,
Their luminescence secrets.
Whispers of worlds beyond our own.
And there, amongst this celestial dance,
Paper moons gently sway.
In rhythms orchestrated by the wind.
With a pen and paper in hand,
I attempted to capture this nocturnal wonder.
Words flowing in ink-soaked cascades,
Trying to balance the essence.

A Mermaid Sleeps

Her heart in shipwrecks.
Tales of adventure,
Forever wanders the sea's vast embrace.
Sometimes recalling woeful tales.

Her soul entwined.
Her song is a timeless saga.
Within the moon's soft glow.
In endless quests, her love still beguiles.

Upon the rough-hewn rocks, her refrain beats.
A melody that every echo reverberates.
Through shadowed caves, her voice dutifully greets.
The world above with haunting,
lips of salt.

Soul In The Dirt

Beneath the loamy surface lie
The roots of ancient wisdom.
Yearning for sunlight.
It harbours stories of bygone days,
Witness to rebirth and decay.
The echo of footsteps.
Etching tales of generations out of step.

Witches

Through the endless, celestial, infinite.
They embrace the cosmos, unfurling souls.
Navigating with certainty and confidence,they fear no bounds,
Their spirits roam.
Mystical, unseen, silent.
Dark as night, they imbibe the moon's pale light,
Mingling with earth's flowing life blood.

Dream Of Dreams

In caverns
Figures play enigmatic games,
Cloaked.
Dreaming of dreams.
Their nimble steps are tethered.
As they juggle moonlit orbs.
Their gestures breathe life.
Creating tapestries of wonder and whimsy.
In my sleep's embrace, I am held enthralled.
By the enigmatic mystique of these harlequins,
For in their eyes, I find reflections.
A kaleidoscope of emotions.

Quietude

No crowded theatre, no endless echoes.
No starlight to blind eyes, piercing.
Only the rustlings of ancient leaves,
A dance of shadows.
Peace nudges my weary bones,
For in this primordial stillness,
Everything becomes a joyful hush.
The quietude—
The nursemaid of feral sleep.

Under Ice

Hopes, like leaves, quiver, fade.
Spinning dreams and madness.
Cyclical roars of silent beats.
Light's dance departs on cue,
Charts, graphs, and life's syllabus drift down, ignored.
Intrusive fumes don coats.
Breath; mimicry in grim shadows is stored.
Chaos commands as dreamers' slumber deepens,
Sweet permanence is their final dream to keep.
A call to rise simply steepens.
The tension; gears grind.
Eyes weary, peering through reality's lens;
Hands fumbling to bring the blurred world to sense.
The others wait in Steel's cold, silent throne.
Above, the clear day holds no clues of
fathoms deep.

Anonymity

Behind their masks, the ghosts of the city,
Their eyes, shattered orbs unmoored,
Drifting past time's relentless tick
Now, in razor-sharp clarity,
Scutting crabwise in a distorted waltz.
Among the thronging junctures, they dance,
Weaving their steps with the precision of a predator,
A ballet painted on the canvas of the streets
Infant giggles pierce the murmur.
A lover's clasp defies the void,
A psyche shatters in cacophony,
A life is snatched within the creeping shadows.
Souls, trapped within the shards of a splintered reflection,
Jostled and lost within the tumultuous wave,
A doorway gapes,the urban beast breathes out.
The world sighs, unshackled yet bound.

Cherished

Wake up from dreams, said the angel.
And put on your silk gown and ghost.
Relate to the fields and forests.
Holding hands with ancestors,
Whose spirits became eternal.
Dancing between sunbeams,
Within twilight's fade to prayer.
Whispering all your memories.
As a lifetime stutter, beware.
Yet when the feasting and hugging have burned,
With untidy, unravelling threads.
Rest a weary head upon cherished pillows,
And reminisce within eternal feather beds.

Kiss The Velvet

In summer's tranquil arms, we find our rest.
As sweet lips kiss velvet.
The sun brightens peeping clouds.
Each caress heals weeping despair.
Lovers' shadows merge as such.
Blesséd rain is now gone.
Leaves earth in solace bare.

The Turning Key

When fairies dance and nymphs cavort,
The air is steeped in earth's wild, fragrant scent.
Each nostril fills, we sense the turning key.
Seasons' shift that stirs the slumbering light.
Behold the creatures, brisk with urgent cheer.
As they prepare for winter's looming kiss.
Nestling treasures,
Past the ridge,
Where the future shadows hide.

Unspoken

In the fertile silence, it bloomed.
Amidst this quiet symphony, each note,
A sentence.
Cradling thoughts yet unspoken,
Tender in their hidden craters.
Nestled in my heart's garden,
Where secret wishes flower.

Within A Dream

In lamb-wool softness, she roamed,
Nursed on the emotive draft of the dance,
In the cradle of imagination.
To rest within his arms,
Who sang upon her lips above the lake?
Her hands cradled nectar, a woven contraband.
Of liquid fire and froth, dry as bone in the sun,
Mingling to sear their polished tryst.
Doubt, a discarded serpent skin, lay in the past.
As ripples toyed within her spirit.

Soul Wanderer

Scour their gazes, ablaze with starlight,
Plumbing depths,
A brief engulfment before they spat back.
Into the spray of tomorrow, untouched by regret.
No mournful love, nor earth-tied passions,
Blunted and dulled.
A devil's voice I play, whispering frostbitten,
My counsel:
"Rebel against the chain of norms."
"Reform before the morning crowds."
Now that the light bleeds, I forfeit my loft.
I wager on the robin.
To seek amnesty.

Salty

In heaving winds,
The sea's deep secrets spill.
Seeking solace in the sands of time.
Waves play against the hardened shore.
Spraying stones with salty kisses.

Where Shadow's Dance

In the cadence of darkness, desires entwine.
Melodies birthed by a celestial vow.
Each step is an echo of forbidden design.
As shadows sway to the rhythm of now.
Dancing in harmony, their souls aflame,
Chasing the moon in elusive delight,
Lost in a dance that's both wild and tame,
Where love's whispers bloom,
Fears take flight.

Angel's On The Lawn

Angels stalking the consecrated grass,
Trampling the dawn's moisture.
And shadows, trailing robes of shimmer and dimness.

The soil sighs beneath their weightlessness.
Their feet are drawing the sacred circles unseen.
They weave—the restless twisters—in the sun's seething bath,

Eddies of bliss, unstitched and re-threaded,
Sending spirals and wishes into the glow-worm night,
While the avian chants, fling prisms into the climb.

Breaths of the earth, in secret, spill
Arcane courage and murmurs of hope
Into the ears of dormant lives,
Enshrouded under the firmament's tapestry.

This hour unfolds, an altar of tranquility,
For peace, a vigilant shepherdess exhales
Her hallowed benediction with each pirouette,
Kissing the day sacred with lips of eternity.

Erebus

In the shadows cast by the moonlight's fading glow, there
    lurks a figure.
His presence whispers secrets, veiled. A realm where light
    and hope begin to fade.
Erebus, princely ruler of the night, Enrobed in witches, his
    soul is mysterious.

Within the realm void of celestial light, he navigates the
    paths most would forsake.
With eyes aglow, he prowls the twilight's haze.
A master of the art of unseen grace.

His steps are shrouded, silent as the breeze. He moves through
darkness while the world's asleep. In dreams, he dances with
his faithful kin. Within the depths of sombre solitude.

His kingdom thrives in shadows. Yet it holds a beauty few
    would dare include. This is not the time to lose your nerve.
Erebus still shines despite his gloom.
Forever.

Visions

Angels meandered on sacred green, twirling amidst the
    dawn's fresh squash, with ribbons of light and dusk.
Unshod, unburdened,
Their dance refined beneath the gaze of mortals,
While birds with vibrant plumes engage.
The breeze hushed,
Carried advice to slumbering spirits beneath the celestial skies.
Serenity prevailed, thus being born, and with tender fervour,
All benedictions were signed.

Words

As breath smelt the snow,
Moonlight words were exposed.
In waterfront bars,
Where promises fed the crowd,
Pecking the thoughts of wordsmiths
As poetry spoke,
Reflecting on the time of childhood,
Romancing yarns
With sock-less adventures in dreams.

Winter Moon

As the frigid air wraps itself beneath sleep.
Footprints fade into the freshly fallen snow.
A path winding through the crisp fields.
Leading me to lands yet unexplored,
Where dreams dance with this seasonal freeze,
As it casts shadows upon the silent earth.
Where beauty and stillness forever entwine.
I see a winter moon, serene and calm.

Cuckoo

And from their nests the cuckoo leaps.
Lofty dreams of the rational are in Brimstone's rain.
Carnage cloaks the lucid and the just in madness.
Daylight mourns her stolen flames.
As nighttime spins her darkened games,
Handles turned on hope's thin guise,
In escape from salvation,
Extinguished beyond the wise.

In The Wind

Vampires who sinned for pieces of stardust.
Relating tales of long ago.
When they were skyward comets and free.
Locked into magic, wearing colourful blazers.
A fairground extravaganza from the heavens.
Maybe kissing rooftops and filling sleeping minds.
With dreams melting beyond a summer's sweat.

Reflection

With laughter, blossoms, and sweet lemonade,
A spectral harmony, neither seen nor defined,
Yet palpable, like memories gently viewed.
And as the sun sinks, painting the skies ablaze,
This summer ghost emerges from the deep,
Waltzing through fireflies' ephemeral haze,
A phantom ballad, secrets safely sheathed.
Its footsteps tread the dewy evening's cusp.
In fields of thistles, where time takes its toll,
A solitary wanderer yearning to adjust,
To the living world and its impassioned plea.

Bonfire

Winter built a bonfire,
Embers glowed, casting a fiery light
Against the stark landscape.
The wind howled with a chilling melody.
As January performed her fight
Against the frigid night's despair.
Brushing the days with soft kisses, sweet,
As whispers danced upon the breeze,
Drifting.

Fields Of Water

Rippled reflections dance beneath
the endless expanse of watery skies,
where sunlight kisses the tranquil surface,
A gentle caress against liquid realms.

These symphonies of colours, vibrant and alive,
As azure meets sapphire, blending seamlessly,
The water does not discriminate.
Embracing all that dare to step into its world.

A sacred image unfurls before our eyes.
Where reeds sway in the subtlest of breezes,
And lilies blossom beneath golden rays,
Painting a canvas of serenity and peace.

Chiller

Separate me from the wrath of the tempest's greed.
Grant me the clasp of your palm.
Yet, refrain from entombing.
Beneath quicksand's insistent flail.

I can don the guise of lamb, gentle as dawn's whisper.
Or, like an avenging angel, upend your very essence.
Imposing oblivion upon your heart.
I am the wanderer of firmament's unseen trails.

Whirling, cavorting, a tempestuous ballet,
Toppling spires, rending oaks, reaving souls.
Still, I can graze your yesterday, your decades,
With kisses as cold as ice—an airy fiasco, anointing.
Your day is filled with invisible turmoil.

For I, the wind, scrawl the charter of your days.
Bid you bask in summer's lighthearted dalliance.
Or flee into a delirious retreat from fever's blaze.
In the shroud of winter, I breathe my fiery breath.

Transform into a sculptor of frosts, a chiller of bones.
Etching crystals on panes, cloaking
a clear view.

Magic And Wonder

An alchemist's brew, concocted.
Unfading verses summon bygone plays.
A cauldron of twigs and nature's castoffs.
As incense drifts and wanders through the air.
Mesmerising tears to the eyes.
In the moon's embrace, untamed desires are born.
Through incandescent skies, stories come alive.
Unveiling secrets on a moonlit street.

Gaze

Within yesterday's eyes, a blind man sought
Amidst undulating wheat's barren embrace,
Farmers' dreams, as their fields, are left to rot.
Where once was born earth's hearty grace?

A cottage of red, its chimney choked so tight,
Spewed forth remnants of fires past,
Timbers and splinters felt the axe's biting night.

The squire's venture, distant though it may be,
Danced with danger, trespass, and quiet deceit.
Yet in the hush of now, cold's sharp decree,
Brought silence where once heard
It softly beat.

Revelries

They pierced the velvet night, fierce comets high,
In liberty's dance, celestial beings,
Bound by enchantment's weave, hues that defy,
A carnival woven into the night's array.
Patterns of flight in a cosmic waltz aligned
Each flare of a painter's brush on darkened slate,
A tapestry of dreams to life confined,
Gleaming, they spun in fates both small and great.
The sky is their canvas, wide and unconfined.
Lit by their fiery tails of sapphire flame,
Their spectacle, a sonnet, wordlessly signed,
A universe's breath, untamed.
In sweeping arcs, they raged their glory's trail.
A fairground extravaganza.
A silent tale.

Bare The Bones

Ripping the sky's own gravity,
Plunging Neptune's fingers,
Each is a serpent's tongue.
Wet your ankles with winter's gloves.
Landward, they glide, biting the unwary.
Then they retreated, whispering softly.
Their lies,
Expose the earth's raw nerve.
As dry as the kiss of a lover.

Machines

In factories they toil, tireless workers,
Interlocking gears, a symphony of rhythm,
They whir and clank.
A well-orchestrated band,
Creating harmony in industry.
But amidst the marvels lies a haunting truth:
Machines don't feel, they don't yearn.
No heart that beats, no soul that dreams,
In their cold embrace, humanity wanes.
They bring us closer, transcending distance.
Buzzing wires, transmitting our thoughts,
Invisible threads connecting our souls,
A web of interwoven existence.

Silently

A silver spearhead in the darkness.
It tears the night open, revealing.
The bones of the earth.
Casting shadows on the canvas.

Each footstep, a whisper of ancient rituals,
Murmuring secrets through the silence
Of the sleeping woods.
As I navigate the labyrinth,
Of mystery and dreams,
A dark language of the heart murmurs.

Promises brood in the shadows,
Like the silken wings of night butterflies.
A tender embrace,
Raw, primal, like a wolf's,
Soft laughter, echoes of bygone times,
A light cuts through, brightening.
Joy sparks like cold steel.

Dust

Each grain is a universe.
A story left untold,
Carried through corridors of space.
Whisked away by lunar winds,
Scattered across dusty plains,
Pure poetry concealed,
In these delicate particles.

Fireflies

In the depths of night,
A flickering light ignites.
Fireflies romance,
Casting their shimmering theatre.
A waltz of nature.
Tiny lanterns.
Ablaze in the darkness.
Guiding souls through the ebony canvas.
Myriad little flames shimmer.
That weave and twirl,
Creating ethereal spheres.
A cosmic ballet that mesmerises,
Through midnight meadows.
And moonlit dreams.
They roam.

Scuffed

Old scuffed shoes walked the innocence of youth.
Trudging with frostbite.
Weary satellites gnawed childhood memories,
Maybe ghosts are beyond the slipped horizon.
Entangled in the sinews of relentless dances,
Sails hoist them onto jagged boat rides,
Toward the abyss of elsewhere.

House

I can touch the sky.
And play dirty with the clouds.
kissing the sun,
As streamers of light filter beyond my windows.
I am metal and glass.
My lease is for many years.
And I will not be swayed by rock and roll.
No matter what the band sings.

Clocks

Apathy of the empty gallery, as the stalls sang old lang syne,

Swigging script empties, lit by candles flickering shadows.
The old deer of pomp and glory, antlers brittle and rose-
thorned, held on to a withering rose, turning nightshade
venom, seeping whispered sheets of music hall bygones.

These phantoms, long unshackled from elsewhere.

Returned to walk the aching boards, echoing their once
fleshly glories—newcomers shivered under the curtains'
wooden applause, A hushed groan, a chill rattle of chains,
frightening even the fiercest heart.

Renewal

Kissing the lips of a butterfly,
They turned away from the twinkling.
Watching fish swim before their eyes.
Boats in the clouds unfurled wide sails,
Boasting their deepest blue.
Streaming across open wilderness in a canvas desert,
They knew that creativity had summoned fresh days.
Sleep not, but touch the quill and paper.
For now, it was time for renewal.

Gathering

The gathering ensues as a new dawn floats into view.
Winter gnashes its teeth and withdraws.
Cuckoos carve the air with haunting calls.
Little robins shed blood-red cloaks,
And lambs spring into the abyss of existence.
Flowers lurch forward, drunk on thawing light.
While hay fields undulate, tiny kingdoms for dormice,
Where poets, unburdened, feast on the world's tender
    green breath.
Streams surge into torrents, and silver spirits strain toward
    the ocean's maw.
High above, gliders cleave the sky.
In the talon grip of thermals, ghost fingers of
the ether.

Whisper

As whispering love sonnets read their notes,
Fingers caressed wavy hair.
Their scarlet ribbons were flowing in the wind.
Applause from beneath silk gowns,
As flesh and bone, previously cold as marble,
Awoke to life.
Unshackled from the doubt of yesterday,
Drinking season's spring,
Breathing into the lungs is as blessed as any beginning.

Glass

Within the reflection,
A face.
A mirror image.
A perfect replica.
Eyes gaze back.
Twinkle.
A spark.
A vision that sees the light.
Into the looking glass,
Beyond the glow of skin and bone,
Into the soul that dwells.
A glimpse that time calls its own.

Breath Of The Wind

For the breath of the wind,
Disturbs clouds.
Making me dream of long ago,
As memories kiss the day,
And party on till dawn's flickering light.
With fire sticks to keep embers smouldering.
Beyond horizons, souls peep,
Awaiting their moment,
To fulfil new beginnings.

Misty Dawn

As the nightingale sang to my lips—
A daggered note pierced through the dusk.
With the spirits of ancient earth.
Surrounding empathy's embrace,
Where breaths salivate in the air.
Beyond faded stars, the ghosts of ancients,
Twinkling—
Their whispers trickle light years,
Summoning depths of untamed
cosmos.

Ripples

As thoughts yawn and rise,
Telling tales from yesterday's Jack Daniels.
Spitting out chiffon and lace,
Lovers twirl and wrestle.
The bird song taunts.
Air loft breezes,
As a swan teases a lake.
Little ships bid adieu,
While angels leaving their shifts return home,
To the kitchen flat line,
Breathing lattes and cappuccinos.

As A Child

I want to dream.
Performing make-believe.
Chasing puppy dog tails.
Touching the clouds.
Kissing the moon.
As my lips taste angel dust.
A rainbow shines.

I Am The Dawn

Wildflowers, those delicate sentinels, awaken; their unseen
senses quiver, reaching feebly for the newborn day.
Ground dwellers erupt from hidden lairs, secretive and
swift; their emergence is a ballet of survival.
Now, a grandstand of breath, each gasps a struggle, each
scent an affirmation of being, as the raw odour of life
surges in the primal air.

Where Cannons Roar

In the field where war ends lives,
A symphony of chaos blooms, and the earth implores.
Peace.
The ground and canvas were splattered red.
And men like brush strokes.
Clash with hearts of lead.
Mirrored in steel.
Anchored to the earthen womb.
Resting.
The guardians of unleashed fury.
Silent sentinels.
Awaiting scorched breath,
Trapped in the twilight of thunderous dreams.
Smoke and ash billow, obscuring the sky.
Unleashing chaos.
An orchestrated nightmare.
In the fields, the artillery
weeps.
Endless.

Revived

Awaken and shake your jangling.
As determination blazes into the hunt, seizing the
forbidden jubilee.
Endless reverie ruptures its shell, and raw wings,
forged anew, storm through myriad thresholds with a
thought's command.
deride the infernal jig and ascend to the celestial symphony.
A spectrum unfurling from darkness to light, the dance pits,
Flee the lunatic's palette, a chaos smeared on fractured nails.
Escape the nightmare's cavern of trial and error,
Rush upon the enchanted battlements, where castles pulse
        with wonder.

Primal

Liquid worlds, bottled, tumble from a basket,
With love bleached clean by moonlit libations,
Entwined in the night's embrace, a constellation
fleeting ecstasy dampened by dawn's foretelling.

Abandonment of doubt—a ship set to sea,
Waves tickling sand-sunken soles,
To feel the raw delight and sensibilities unfurling,
A regress to primal pulse, bare and native.

The Mother Tree

Near the ancient girth of the mother tree,
Her gnarled arms cradle me against winter's raw breath.
The forest's murmured wrath, dampened beneath her
    skeletal embrace,
She shields me from the night's feral glee.
A midnight whisper of frost snakes through the air.
Crafting a spectral panorama of unnatural delight.
I nestle deep within her background sanctuary.
Better this woodland womb than the wastelands of shadow.
Owl eyes blink, predator-proud, dissecting the dusk.
Beaks and talons, death's silent apostles, seek their suffering
    feast. Unseen, I lie, heart bone thudding within the
    timber's ribs,
Temptation to flee to cottage covert chokes in my thoughts.
Phantom breath and woodland sprites
Weave mischief in this nocturnal theatre,
Valhalla reimagined in whispers,
Their agonised applause, a silent storm, as the mother tree
    holds me still.

At The Skies Demise

Scratching at the skies' demise.
Water, rising from the briny deep,
Salt devoured by the gust,
Hung suspended like a breath,
Creeps between the blink of your eyes.
Vapour-flecked, the tongue's taste bites,
Sprinkled shards from heaven's reach,
In a phantom's soft communion with dust.
Each flake a ghost flitting away. —
The wanton wind, lustful in its grasp,
Painter of a desolate symphony,
Whispers of an icicle dance.
All white, a crust of brittle purity,
Virgin Earth's unspoiled quilting,
Sullied soon by the tracks of the wandering,
Gander spoils the soft romance.
With trespassing feet.

Night Owls

The light's molten kiss trickles down the iron jaw.
On the horizon, unfreezing the sky's steel grip.
Listening to the raindrops feeding the hoi polloi.
Rain's fingers tap their coded Morse onto leaves.
Mud stirs, roots drink deep, and the secret gospel
Of the waterfall, as life hums in the undergrowth.
Dancing with the insects whose wings flutter by.
In the muse of the gnats, the air's whispered symphony,
Fragile as spun glass, an emperor's mandolin
Splintered over the earth.

Echoes

As endless echoes haunt each empty vessel,
Their spirits linger here, so lost and frail.
The remnants of their lives, now but a breath,
The tales untold, the secrets they conceal,
Yet in this limbo, they may find some rest.
Yet still they wander, echoes of the past,
For in these cerebral halls, their souls will last.

Over The Plain

Its silver glow,
A beacon of the night,
Its aura is floating gently.
As a shawl, embracing all beneath its clouds.
Its tones are soft, with an eerie melody.
A harmony that echoes over the plains,
The distress rustling, in rhythmic horror,
A lullaby for the masses.

Embrace

Tales of ice in their eerie embrace,
From those who haunt the land, it seems,
Their ethereal forms fill the space.
As chaos within your lair.
They glide across the blanket spread.
Their ghostly touch upon your skin,
And as you lie within your dreams,
Their gentle hum begins.

Twilight

As dawn kissed twilight goodnight,
And folded blankets of clouds upon the horizon,
The wind socks blew west.
As the last of the stars left the stage,
And they switched off their lights.
Becoming shy and blank.

Hidden Path

The dying light embraces earth in a song.
The day's events are put to rest by weeping,
As silence becomes the time to right each wrong.
Foretelling the arrival of the night,
The world begins to slip into a dream.
A cloak of darkness shrouds each hidden path.
Yet, in this darkness,
Love still finds a way.

Tantrums

Whispers from the gallery,
As they shield their appetite,
By allowing melting hearts to skip a beat,
In that place, called beyond.
Whining its way through the ears,
Split with the drums of feasting dawn.
Maybe the stomping or tantrums of the undead,
Chained to eternity,
As they yell at Beelzebub.
What oatmeal is being cooked now?

Muse

At this moment, I found my muse,
And my soul danced within perfection.
As art and music sang till dusk,
Reflections rose above the moon.
So in the silence of the night,
I keep this memory close.
In dreams,
I'll hear the art that's bright.
And let it guide my soul.

All That Jazz

And as dust,
A wandering breeze's friend,
Endlessly drifting through the open air,
Without a purpose, a journey has no end.
Traversing lands through valleys.
A force, unseen but felt in every way.
A whisper on the skin.
A brush of breath mingling with scents
In the morning at play.
Exchanging secrets with nature.
No weight, no anchor,always on the move.
There is no burden to tie it down.
Nor a chain.
Life's mysteries dance to the groove.
Of hope, freedom,
All that jazz.

Fragrance

Kissing under the violet's sweet perfume,
The dandelion whispered it's refrain:
Their love burst forth as spring's first bloom,
A joy that soared beyond earthly pain.
The rose's fragrance draws them near and dear.
Their love bond is eternal,something no one can sever.
With each new dawn, their love becomes clear.
Pure devotion that will last forever.
Their love, like the flowers, will never die.
For in each other's arms, they will forever lie.

It Came To Pass

That his great friend, Sir Kit Breaker,
He met his end in a flicker of sparks—electrified,
Changing a plug. The maker summoned him.
"They say his ghost was still smouldering.
When Fireman Bucket arrived," words muttered.
"Hair-raising it must have been!"
"Majorly fried," said the bitter echo.
"Have you come to disturb my grief?"
"What!"
"What are his shoes?
"Those shined in a mirror—size nine, my size—
Another life they might walk with me."
"You wish for his wardrobe next, perhaps?"
The jester voice was in mourning.
"There's treasure in grief, turned trinket hoarder."
"He's gone; these remnants are fleshless now."
"Maybe his spirit will curse the thief, wandering the dark."
"I am no thief! Only shoes, size nine."
"These remnants are not yours."
"They've no need for his possessions; walk him now.
Only spiritual slippers fit."
"And angel wings, you Jest."
"Size nine."
"No."
"What then?"
"Where is his lantern?"
"Lantern?"
"Light for the spectral path."
"He's dead; he needs no lantern."

"The afterlife is dark—forever a shadowed realm."

"But perhaps a torch?"

"A candle?"

"You jest again, jester in grief."

"What of his pledge, our little inheritances?"

"Now is not the time."

"It is.

Entitled are the living to the traces of the dead.

"Later, I'll commune with him. Shall bid for his shoes.

    My size. Size nine."

"No."

Dustbin

Empty as trash,
Hitting the grave.
Without the instruction manual.
Flailing arms salute the daisies.
Air-light legs walk amongst the debris,
Broken eyes watch their sunset
With quivering lips.
And tearing off a strip of bandages,
As life rolls over,
Ever asking why.

And Angels Strolled

Fierce-footed, across the sacred turf,
Dancing in the spears of dawn's dew.
With their plumes of light and shadow,
Barefoot and wild, they whirled.
In the scaling crucible of mortal sunlight,
Casting their dreams into fretted eyes.
With brutal, vivid songs,
Breathing into the wind's ear.
Words of marrow-stirring courage.
Unyielding hope.

Off The Port Bow

Mapping realms unmarked.
Listen then to their hymn, see them whirl,
Clothed in eternal tapestry, the weave
Fine as frost's breath, pure as sacred snow,
They descend, swift as hawks,
Gentle as a mother's touch.

Fairies And Nymphs

The air, tattooed with the musk of the untamed,
Bites the nostrils with the wild's raw essence—
seasoned gasp as the earth's skin tightens.
Beasts and fowl scurry, bustling as mad architects.
Their claws and beaks laden with winter's hoard.
Before the cold boulders roll over the horizon.

Wild Flowers

The last wildflowers, fevered relics,
Raise their petals in defiant salute
To the melancholy wind's bleak lull.
Even the clouds, those sagging ancients,
Weep glistening tears to baptise the day,
While a feeble, blushing sun stumbles,
Trying to coax warmth into a dying landscape.
Berries burst with the sickly promise of decay.
Leaves spiral in their terminal dance.
The final gasp of the harvest bleeding into the soil.
A master's hand, deliberate and cruel,
Paints the scene with grandeur and dusk.
Autumn grins, a mischief beneath Toil's mask,
Weaving dreams steeped in darkening light.

Revelations

I don't want to sleep in my dreams.
I want to wrestle with the molten sun.
Its heat is prying open my lips.
While the world's heartbeat drums.
I want to inhale the raw essence of summer's fervour,
To exude an ancient hymn, soothing my soul,
As serene and potent as the butterfly's ballet.
Yet, beneath this peace, shadowed beasts stir, whispering
    the secrets of primal wars.
Mangled leaves twitch.
The forest's breath quivers under their confessions.
Through the tangled thorns,
The blood of ages bleeds into roots.
Feeding darkened
revelations.

Lanterns In Nocturne

Night's velvet shawl, bejewelled with winks of sleep,
Silent whispers of cosmic lore, each a quiet invitation.
Moon, a solitary sentinel, stands guard, aloof,
Illuminating dreams spilled beneath her silver roof.
Stars stitch the ebony quilt with celestial light.
Guiding weary travellers through the waltz of delight.

Teddy Bear

My little bear had one eye. The right one.
And one ear. The deaf one.
When you turned him upside down, he spoke very oddly.
My name is Rapscallion; he would like to think.
And I have magic within my little chest.
It got lodged there after a wizard had been swallowed.
And washed down after far too much porridge brunch.
He was like this. A bit bear-like.
At the toy factory, he had gone into the abstract pile.
Actually, he remained there for quite a while.
Yet when all the other bears were going to sleep,
And he shushed them not to peep.
He would go down to the shop floor and do his pirouette.
Howling at the moon,
His beige form would sing as well as a bear could.
He would glance and so swoon that he was magical, fun,
And it should not have been rejected and undone.
So it was the golden slippers that appeared.
Magic was dispatched to surprise.
And coughing a maelstrom,
The bear did wing it.
To fly away, up into the sky.

Scarecrow's Two

Straw heads displayed pennies in their eyes.
No tears to reminisce about other playful games,
Or cycling over the hills,
As their overheating bodies burst into flames,
And said adios, and skyward blew.
Yet now they had a second chance.
To maybe romance, as their hats doffed the brow,
With blank expressions, looking at lost horizons,
As they quickly ran off into fields of corn and barley.
Their mouths breathed in heaven's grace.
Swallowing in the cool air of autumn,
Playing with dancing circles,
With arms clenching their alter egos.

Tiger Moth

Maybe his Tiger Moth would remain airborne.
Fueled by tears dried upon bedroom pillows.
To scatter memories over poppy fields.
No ice cream or jam rolls today.
Angels had carved a eulogy,
To welcome new bones.
For downwards, he spun and stuttered.
Field clocks had lost their spring step at four p.m.
Rowlf the dog, bowed his head.
His master had enrolled in the unknown.

Chronicles

The king had breathed his last on this splendid winter's morning. Ice bathed the land in their castles and keeps. The lawyers of the deceased had paper-weighted his instructions to the loyal fiefdom. The incantations of yesterday feel forlorn now upon this shivering January day. The very veins of blood that ruled the land had dried and turned to sand beneath riverbeds of soot after years of battle, and shields and giants upon horseback were acting their thoughts to cleanse the breath of change blowing from the north. Statues personified their weary frosts, whose stare glanced at all compass points. Snowflakes danced with the moon as arrows of deeds swallowed the warmth for perhaps eight weeks, but when the southern seas froze at the shore edge, then the sun's rays and it itself would slumber and hide until further notice. Wolves roamed the land, and deer bones lay where slaughtered by nature, as tiny creatures ventured not upon snowdrift blankets. Coldness fettered even the stones as hither and thither went the clothed autocracy of state, as they hid their feelings and squealing, as they saddled their emotions with thoughts as unpalatable as their hearts feared the coming of the king's son, who all said "would eternal winter be." Yet for now, the chronicles of the dead king would ring church bells up and down the land as all would prepare for the coming dance of Maelstrom.

Field The Artillery

General Blink sat in the field, awaiting orders to obey.
Bacon and chips, he thought, were the enemies' play.
Cursing his retirement had been put on hold till dawn.
Then he could return to Mayhem.
All pulverised within the lawn.
Yet it was a timber-framed affair.
All sitting beneath a parapet with binoculars to stare.
Old Simonds Stump and Colonel Frosty Fries,
Both had eaten shrapnel, both taken by surprise.
Both had thrown in their mince pies and potato peelers as
well. Some had lobbed a cocktail of chicken,
And pineapple chunks from hell.
Boozy had slung his schnapps from Fritz in 1913.
A year before the slaughter evolved,
Yet his friend was nowhere to be seen.
Bully beef and wafers,
But mostly communion, dust, and grain.
Old Curly Slugger had fired artillery.
And they thought He was to blame?

Rendezvous

In days of yore, where seafarers dwelt and legends bright
  were spun,
A tale emerges from the froth, a different conquest,
  one less won.
"I am no Sir Francis Drake," comes a voice from shores
  uncharted.
"And you, not a galleon fierce and bold, yet from sea to
  heart departed."
Stolen ships and battered dreams, needle in the compass spun,
Your marbles in my brain are echoes of the victories won.
Shouts and laughter interwoven, a tapestry of jest unfurled,
And Neptune, buoyant name, adrift in the sea as your
  laughter swirled.
Our rendezvous, a tangled web, love's quest in want of prose,
Not bursting pop nor fizz of joy, but a dance of
  juxtaposition.
Set with furrowed whispers, sour in demeanour quietly spread,
A palette mixed with love's strange hues—tender blue and
  blushing red.
Push me from the seawall's edge; might your eyes in mine
  reflect?
A skyline wide, horizons bend, moments caught in unchecked.
And as I fell, I could whimsy pause to snatch your size fives,
Pawns shop in memory's lane, where secrets are forbidden.
Charm like mighty Boudicca, fierce grace in every stand,
Odin's whispers on my lips; your legend sweeps the land.
Yet herein lies the ungentle truth, the swift ire of your rebuke.
A kick to wake my reverie, love's lesson, bittersweet rebuff.

So let's go to the pub, my dear. The night's youthful
gaze upon us round,
May exit Brahms, may stagger Liszt, as into the mirth
we're bound.
In the joyous gutter's solace, find a toast to the stars
above, untold.
Just "go," the word unsaid, remains; love's tale in
laughter rolls.

Upon Shadows

To you, I am in the darkness, hiding in the shadows, with
     my spotlight turned off.
Let me be here, alive and free.
Listen to the nightingale sing.
I float above the wispy sun and all it brings.
Music feeds my mind with symphonic splendour.
Tender dances,
Upon fulfilled hearts,
Where'll we kiss and embrace till dawn's light?
I whisper as a tease.
Tellingly, in the spring.
Let the cuckoo bring confusion to empty nests.
Two people sit on deck chairs.
Remembering music brings tears to the joy of sound.
Taste the wine; forever is here.
Smileys are a reflection of the day.
Fulfilling all the lovers' grace with excitement.

The Medieval Knight

For who removed the splendor once draped upon my
    shoulders?
And replaced it with torn remnants—a mosaic of a
    beggar's quarters?
No towering bulwarks rise against the sky, no ramparts for
    whispered secrets,
Forsaken, the courtly fools who once adorned my hours
    with jests.

Gone, the feasts that sprawled beneath the glow of self-
    wrought rule,
Stretching back to times of yore, to monarchs who held the
    jewelled sceptre.
Silent now, the halls that echoed with boasts of conquests
    cruel,
And vanished, the hangman's shadow, plotting his next
    eager play.

Treason echoes not within these fields, where solitude's
    weight comes to rest,
Only garlands of indifferent blooms, a mute and fleeting
    company.
No coin clinks for honeyed ale; the innkeeper's snarl—my
    desperate test,
Lodged between the barking hounds' unleashed frenzy and
    diminishing dignity.

Yet I am no jester, fooling with the sharp edge of a
    barbed tongue.
Nor do I bear the stain of guilt that yields under the
    torturer's wringing plea.
Just a sudden pauper by decree, stripped of hearth and
    heartstrings strung,
Cast aside family lineage for the foreign quarrels by the sea.

In The Air

The wind scores its invisible symphony.
Whirling and carving, scripts without ink.
As a hawk's claw etches the sky,
A shaman conjuring scenes of breath and bone.
Eternal hieroglyphs were never erased or lost in the void.
No easel to bear witness, no canvas to hold,
Only the image was born within, erupting into nothing.
Cyclone of living patterns.
One stroke—two strokes—three.
Beyond human sight, a spectre for celestial eyes alone.
Shapes churn and meld as my hands spiral.
Fingers beating their secret drum against the air.

Memories

Time to sheath the deity of conflict,
Don the iron-shod boots, tread the rugged spine of the earth,
Ascend to life's celestial summits.
Bathe in renewal's torrent, cleanse the salt-streaked cheeks,
Beginning anew, lead me to the dawn,
From agony's pit, I will rise.
Bearing my ragged sack of memories,
Images flicker kindly in my mind's theatre.
Behold the robin's red-breasted call,
The thrush's song, the blackbird's cry,
The eagle, with its fierce talon and piercing gaze,
Scales, unseen heights, surveying below
The blooming orchard, the awakening boughs.
No one can tether me now.
I glide through mist, a phantom, a tease.
Mourn not for me upon the staircase of an endless day,
Peace has found me.
Time's relentlessly ticking away.
I am called home to slumber.
To dreams spun by angels' laughter.

Flowers

What are you blowing in the breeze?
Majestic under the brooding canopy,
Your colours, wine-drenched, vivid,
Swaying to the earth's primal rhythms,
A chorus of petals in blood-red and purple,
Your time to burn with the sun's fierce eye,
In the silent dance of Flora, fierce and unyielding.

Can I hear you sing, or is it the wind?
That hums through your slender throats,
As you twist and turn, a wild ballet
In the searing grip of this cloudless drought.
Small yet fierce, proud warriors in the blessed soil,
Fed by the tears of yesterday's fury.

Dream your wild dreams, little flowers,
Before your seeds, scattered soldiers,
Take flight into the unknown,
A new garden to be born, hidden and silent,
In the earth's eternal, violent cycle,
To rise again in forms unseen, untamed.

Sleepy Shores

I am going home washed up on sleepy shores.

As my pain and legends bake into the land.

Sailing my little ship into harbours.

I wave at my ancestors, showering my soul with tears of life.

No anger or guilt,

But grateful for exits now in slumber.

Kissing the rain and showering my clothes.

For sunlight peeking through hurricane clouds,

Dissolves yesterday's experience with tomorrow's unknown.

Misty Dawns

If I should cry myself to sleep under misty dawns.
Undress the curtains and reveal the veiled light.
Wash away the night and turn off burning stars.
Spilt from yesterday's dance beyond sunset.
Sleep as holy memories spear the sky.
Less the cuckoo sings.

Arm In Arm

Let us walk arm in arm,
Towards the nearest shoreline,
And dip our feet in the surf.
With a warm sun above our heads,
Let us remember yesterday,
To link our today,
To tomorrow's hopes and dreams.

Shadows Always Find A Way

They always find a way.
Servants of night's deep monarchy,
They gulp the remnants of our day,
At the pale cusp of the eclipse.

Their tendrils, phantom-wrapped ghosts,
Graze the cheek of now dissolving fireworks,
Soft-easy in the encroaching gloaming,
Where light bleeds into sleep.

For the above atmospheric peek and shut-eye,
Soon withering and pausing in tinged delight,
Dulling fingers streamed in nature's playground,
As time marvelled, displaying her ending script.

Under Cover Of Rain

They arrived under cover of rain.
Cloaked in the downpour's towel.
Sleek bodies weave through the river's heaving nightmare.
Compelled by the relentless currents of the sky and dreams.
Thoughts thrashing—flee, flee from rendering anguish.
Night's agents in the sodden camouflage of storms,
Furtive shapes gliding, meshed with the river's roar.
With the iron pulse of the deluge,rage, funnelled.
Into the torrent's chant—a choir of liquid tumbling.
Minds caught in the watery throes, the swirl and pulse
        of nature's intent.
flee, flee—

The Next Room

If I should release a pauper's breath,
As life ebbs into the next room.
Let me give your moon a kiss.
As I eat my vanity with humble affection.
Melting my shadow into the praying dawn.
Feeling a tepid sun tickle my cheeks,
As angels flex their wings,
I stand in a shoeless embrace.
Binding my memories without and within.

Til Twilight Calls

Dance, oh soul, where daisies nod and sway.
'Neath the sun's caress, just rest and stay.
Life's tapestry weaves.
Spring's silent song is in flight.
Whispers of wind, leaves a hush.
Hear, beating heart, where shadows mask.
The moon's embrace.
In dreams, sweet play.
Till twilight calls, thus night folds to pray.

Shadows

If I bow my head and cry into sand,
Will you dust the shadows from my soul?
And let me rest my bones in your dreams,
As I reminisce about love's lost time.
Shouting at the sky.
Unsure of what just happened?

Ghosts In The Mirror

Each night I hear their spectral footsteps tread.
Their pensive sighs upon the stillness fall.
Their mournful moans, a mournful dirge, they spread.
As endless echoes haunt.
Spirits linger here, so lost and frail.
Remnants of their lives, now but a breath.
Tales untold, the secrets they conceal.
Yet in this limbo, they may find some rest.
Still they wander within their past.
Drowned in empty vessels.
Their souls will dance.

Rolling Hills

Amidst the green and gold,
The rolling hills unfurl their curves and dip with ease.
Soft breezes dance with daffodils and dills.
A sweet escape from life's tumultuous angst.
Peaks and valleys,
A calm symphony of earth and sky.
And all that dwells between their gentle slopes.
This balm makes eyes weary.
Their vast expanse, a surrealistic sea.
Where verdant meadows stretch to meet the horizon.
And tranquil streams weave a path through the land.
A peaceful haven where the soul can fly.
To let go of all that it needs to withstand.

Breath Two

Darkened branches reach for the heavens.
The moon casts its pale light upon the ground.
As a snow-white blanket shines beneath its glow.
But now, that beauty fades without a sound.
As Venus takes her leave, her grace to depart.
The frosty air is sharp against the cheek.
Yet still the deer observe, silent and free.
And like dust, a wandering breeze's friend.
Endlessly drifting through the open air.
Without a purpose, journey without end.
Traversing lands, through valleys.
A force, unseen but felt in every way.
A whisper on the skin, a brush of breath.
Mingling with scents of morning and day.
Exchanging secrets with nature.
No weight, no anchor, always on the move.
No burden to tie it down,
Nor a chain life's mysteries.
It dances to the groove of hope, freedom,
And all that joy.

Spark Of The Moon

The tree-lined view from the bell tower,
Echoed sounds of blessings,
Bringing forth a symphony of grace,
As every soul bowed its head in solace.
Thus, at this moment of serenity divine,
We feel the spark of life,
As the night took flight,
We basked in the glory of the Moon.

Spirit's Of The Night

Sleep beside the spirits of the night,
Their whispers deny sweet reprieve,
This presence alarms, scuttling plight,
And every burden so terrifies.
Tales of ice in their eerie embrace,
From those who haunt the land, it seems,
Ethereal forms fill the space,
As chaos within your lair.
They glide across the blanket spread,
Their ghostly touch upon your skin,
And as you lay upon your bed,
Their gentle hum begins.

Feeling The Moment

Cloudless skies exchange their silent vows.
for poetry that spills from tender mouths,
blessed by the renaissance of daydreams,
over fields of wheat, barley, and lazy sun hats.

Time's clock hopes to recall
summer dances by paddling streams,
where towel-dried feet find bliss
in the tender touch of loving hands,
feeling the fleeting moment gently.

Thrice Ghosts

The ghost shines, illuminating all.
Its silver glow is a beacon of the night.
An aura floating gently as a shawl.
Embracing all beneath its clouds.
It's tones soft, a melody,
Harmony that echoes over the plains.
The distress rustling, in rhythmic horror,
A lullaby for the masses.

Shadows Of Ghosts

Their presence lingers, undeniable.
As shadows waltz in twilight's embrace.
Whispers murmur ancient secrets,
Phantoms glide upon the tapestry of stars.
With held breath, we glimpse their haunting gaze.

Behold spectral forms emerging,
Echoing whispers, blowing as they pass.
Stomping and shaking the very earth,
Marching with fierce, resounding steps.
A passion for music pulses within.

With fervent emotion, they conduct a celestial choir,
Crafting melodies that weave through the night.
Their energy, an inner inferno,
Symphonies resonate and echo beyond time.

Scent

Sweet lavender kisses,
As daisies bloom in fields of gold,
With dreams so wispy that scent the atmosphere,
Whispering ambience, soft lullabies told,
To float away to saffron and silk pastures.

Starlit night with paper moons,
Whispering ghosts,
Fearsome,
Rivers flowing in eternal light,
Embers glow as fireside breathes,
Calming fragrance fills the air.

Dying Light

The dying light embraces earth in song.
As twilight weaves its veil of whispered hush,
And silence beckons forth each soul's remorse.
Foretelling night's embrace, the world grows still,
In the shadows' dance, a dream unfolds unseen,
Where paths entwine through realms of deepest night,
Yet love persists, a beacon undeterred.
Though veiled, its essence lingers in the air.
Entrancing hearts with whispers of its might,
Binding them in bonds cannot break,
Enthralled by passion's spell,
They Surrender.

Brush Strokes

At this moment, I found my muse,
As my soul danced within perfection,
For art and music, sing till dusk.
Reflections rose above the moon.
In the silence of the night,
To keep this memory close,
In dreams, I hear the art that's bright,
And let it guide my soul.

Mrs.Savage Pickled Dandelions At Noon
(Alternative version)

Mrs. Savage pickled dandelions at noon in the fierce
    meadows, where nature crowns herself Queen.
She, the alchemic empress of the moment,
Her spoils have been triumphant yet arduous.
Playfully breathing shadows at dusk.
Speckled hands dug between May and June.
Yellow leaves released and jar filled,
To begin a new holistic venture.
This journey is not of distance but of date-stamped experience.
Mrs. Savage traversed the calendar where weeks respire—
As her toil and sweat, pendulum in perfection, resonates in
    the tick and tock,
Governed by the kiss of nymphs and fairies.
Their breath is seeding new ground for the process to begin
    again (eternal).

On The Moon There Lived A Cat
(Alternative Version)

On the moon, there lived a cat.
Lives count nine, amidst the wild dust,
Nine lives to tender beyond the cratored rust.
She prowls, whiskers tuned to the cosmic tide,
Alone with the stars bestowed her cunning side.
A creature of shadow,
She leaps, a canine trick as a floating ballet.
Her appetite is alive, scavenging every day.
Nine beats of the heart where the mysteries dance,
A feline deity, a moon mariner's romance.
Beneath her gaze, solarfish dare not tread.
For she keeps a diary of littered dead,
And weaves her silence in the starless of night,
Milking this cold empty light.

She Painted Other People's Dreams
(Alternative Version)

She painted other people's dreams,
Poleaxed by the summit of imagination.
Here, in such a bleeding storm,
Burnt the weeping willows, whose silent domain,
Holds the sorrow of images in landscape.
Shaman dripped.
She caught them: the wild, the wistful, the screams.
On canvas, nightmares and fantasies.
A montage of playful vengeance.
Seeking redemption from the apex of sleep.
Yet, who steals the dreams of the dreamer?

We Gathered At The End Of Time
(Alternative Version)

We gathered at the end of time.
Clawed from the fraying edges, we huddle,
A floating ballet without a script
Ragged at the close-shut gates of nowhere.
Dusty, gasping at the mocking void.

'Tis a healer we summon, a shaman or a doctor.
To stitch the sinews of our spent cosmos.
Perhaps fables surround these terminal breaths,
Perhaps redemption lurks—a mysterious outcome.
Memory-heavy with salvation unseen.

Aye, but our tale swerves, snarled and ensnared,
Among the roots of retelling.
A maze of whys woven into the very earth.
To lose and find ourselves endlessly.
No meaningless words in this tale, however.

Yesterday I Fell Asleep
(Alternative Version)

Yesterday I fell asleep into the abyss.
As light bled its last on the hem of the day,
Dusk unfurled its russet coat and slipped,
Beneath the door of consciousness.
There, in the dark lair of night, unmoving,
Where hours wove their silky threads 'round my form,
I was swallowed whole by that gaping chasm.
Missing the silent reminder.
I did not linger in the twilight's spectacle,
Nor did I hear the nightjars' mystic calls.
I bypassed the rites of nocturnal creatures,
And the whispers of shadows playing on walls.
Until dawn, in her waking grace,
Stretched her rosy fingers, teasing the night,
Coaxing my eyes to flutter open and witness.
This world is reborn in her soft, gentle light.

Beneath The Moonlight

Upon that hill, she sang the sweetest song imagined. There beneath the moonlight upon that warm summer's eve. As wispy clouds rolled home to bed. A late-phase setting where angels smiled and fed. Music sublime and gentle rolled into earshot. And nature responded with joyous peace. All relaxed, where angst was banished to lose. Little starlings flew overhead and swirled in games of joy. And humans lay back in each other's arms, having kicked off their migraine blues. As Firefly's and others demonstrated that this had been a truly wonderful day.

Miss Debonair

So, there she stood, all propped up with gin.
Dancing in the cornfield, playing her violin. Stoking the
rest of a musician's lament. Harping upon the triangle of a
youth misspent. Abstract words within this crafted tune.
A masterpiece with the spiritual choir to sing the rhyme.
It was all bursting with synergy, especially from bottled
wine. Accompanied by a cello and piano that argued for the
rights of finesse. Miss Debonair had abandoned delusion
and created a symphonic success. Standing in her bare feet
as shoes had holed too much. Her gown of dressing for the
crowd is now clothed in sounds emanating free. The silence
of her crafting mind had opened her soul to be.

Feather And Dusted

My pillow has just woken, and all the Neanderthals have clubbed my dreams. Sweating insistent that floating feathers are definitely out to breakfast. I was yawning with the dawn as we happily flirted at six am, with the light soothing my eyes via the open curtains that faced due east. The larks seem to be laughing well this morning. Tugging at my ears to get up and glance through the window and taste a peek at their playful nuisance. Shuffling like a clown in a duvet, I so missed my silence and stumbled into breakfast life, cursing the fact that sleep had thus ceased, and it was now time for my body clock to alarm my bones into a semblance pose.

Rest A While

Yet you sit pondering your account without shouting
and not giving the game away. For savour, the moment
and blink your cries, for now, is the twilight of your ever-
dissolving day. I see a mist swirling into embrace as its
form appears familiar as it springs from yesterday's family
tree. Thus, it smiles and beckons a wave and says, Tarry
my friend and come on this journey with me. Into the
unknown and beyond the sky, and yes, the stars as galaxies
are not a hindrance but a warm spinning disc of dust and
cloud. As if majestically building your shroud. More birds
in the trees twitter, their sounds as messengers perhaps,
as your time thus lapsed, and so away into their world of
treetops rest. For you have now gone away invisible, at
peace till times end, and always to be your best.

The Soul Wanderer

Look at me with my ethereal body floating above this misty grace. Whispering sweet nothings as I loop and swoop with pace. Staring at the milk beams of a moonlight trail to flavour. I therefore stake my claim on landscapes' winter behaviour. Snowdrops, not rain, gain my gratitude for linking arms with my soul and pointing ever to distant lands of sleepy hamlets with life in a hush of a tale of subdued delight. I am in the air, floating as a dare, perhaps above trees with all and sundry below. As they gallop on horseback or swat their thoughts for a simple out-of-body experience called dreams. I can witness their starlit eyes looking into distant hollows, which swallow them briefly, before chiefly settling away to spray their future quests with no regrets of failed love or distant romance floored to grounded level. Perhaps I play the devil's advocate and whisper in their frozen ears to behave, not to be a slave to behaviour but to try and reform. Maybe before dawn as I let go of my soaring height and do gamboles with the robin who chirps a good day to my way before retreating to my home's carefully prepared lodge. Now I must dodge one with all, as I have a single call to wake Molly by the pool to beckon her to arise from the deep. So, refuse her slumber to sleep. Thus, join me as the soul's wanderer, to be at nature's pace and law. As I always have for centuries before. So, with a sweep of my hand, but nothing really grand, my breath fills the air with ambiance and flair as I dance a waltz with new wings in my bow, perhaps. Nothing to lapse and dawdle here then that orchestrated sounds cannot relay. A look, a glance, a kiss, a smile—life thus returns to breath to exist without any hindrance for a while.

Swing Me Your Bones

Swing me your bones, and I will sing you a lullaby. Together we shall drink the nectar juice of flower petals on tap. Perhaps even read the sonnets of our elders, who tread this path to immortal dances. Twirling with silk bind and thread, as gentle as any spun web of complex homes. Rest a while hence and feel the wind fleece your soul with warm strength and admission. To the outer gate of above cosmos height, flying and wing napping, running your fingers and toes into adventures not yet been. A lift into that bubble wraps home of an ancestral dream.

In The Asylum

Listening to the feedback from the asylum as the lunatic flew the ceiling. Passing his warped marbles upon the baying crowd below as they sat in their electric chairs awaiting the coming of the rains. It was that apocalyptic moment as all the cuckoos flew the nest and came to rest upon the memories of Jack, a Victorian who walked his East End and strangled the night with murder and mayhem. It was the deconstruction of sanity as the padded cells flung open their hell's and rang their bells as fire and brimstone stung the lofty aspirations of the sane and doused them in the carnage of the mad. Daylight had thus lost her candles, and nighttime had turned the handles of hope as the only place left to flee was away from him.

Lies

Slowly I sit upon my hands, awaiting for the freedom bell to ring in my head, as I tread a straight and narrow path. Fleeing from the enemies' curse as it performed worse than the angels in the devil's kitchen. Yet I have said I will be free and maybe strike a bargain with myself if I can be left in peace and chase them to the cliff edge and watch them fall via gravity to the rocks below and place their bones on the rocks of their master's demise.

Mr Elastic

For he had wandered into the hills to see the floating butterflies as gravity had ceased a spot. Mr. Elastic had thus reached the horizon quickly and looked back to see his giant steps gawking towards his position. Mayflies danced in circles as tree-hogging birds could loop the loop in slow motion. The flowers, soil strapped, did not float away, but pollen, seeds, and others did leave their ground and reach waist height upon this odd day before advancing into the sky, distracting an eagle, who had majestically reached the stratosphere. For Mr. Elastic, a pole vault over a fence had leapt him to near cloud height before gambolling back to ground and laughing at his predicament. Other animals did not walk but hovered with useless feet or hoofs and made sounds that reacted to their unease. For others, however, it was such a tease and a breeze, as the wind's breath swirled gently in any way she pleased. Even the clouds could be pushed away to circumnavigate the sun, which was unfamiliar, and dressed as a simple football-sized red button. The ambiance for Mr. Elastic as he leapfrogged over a small village with its confused inhabitants holding onto normality and sanity perhaps, by their fingernails, made him forever laugh and wonder why.

Samhain

Were they once not women or also men? Faces distorted within the clocks of time. Their groaning moans bellowed into the fields and spooky lanes, where ghosts and spectres walked, and legions of bones lined their history with years of marching boots, so well-worn and treading their routes. Centuries uncleansed with turmoil unleashed. Creaking and sounding as hallows gone mad. Coming for the living to admonish deep sadness. Slowly sinking into fever, their conquest of delusion was thus complete, as they billed their lack of empathy into attacking sweetness and delight.

Stumps

He knew his innings were coming as soon as the bails got hit. Perusing in his flannel whites, he had to stand, not sit. With a bat in hand, he strolled out to the middle and passed the bowler, Fleece. The other fellow had caught a duck as he stumbled at the crease. Adjusting his senses, he patted the ground and looked around the field. To clear the boundary ropes, he thought and hit it to the crowd. All those laughing in the stands would surely think him proud. A hop, a skip, and a mumble sent all hopes flying far. It was a lonely retreat, he thought, as his optimism said, "Hoorah!"

Chronicles (Act Two)

For who removed the glitter and gold and replaced them with rags and tags? No more turrets and castles to rampart walk and fools within reach to choose to dress my day. What of the banquets and spoils of self-made laws going back to King William or Athelstan himself? No more carpet bragging or hanging assassins who failed. Yet not treason but to wake up in a field with only garlands of flowers as friends. And they refuse to talk anyway.

No coin for ale, and the keeper says be gone, or the dogs will dementedly be let free, to rascal my dignity. But I am no halfwit who befuddled his play of words and destroyed the King with a verbal lashing. Nor the rack to tumble out any guilt or nonsense. Simply to awake to a decree taking my lands and property and sons, daughters, and wife to destitute for losing battles overseas. Yet to take revenge, you need more than one egg in a basket. For I rode on with only a handful of dutiful men, and all are gone now. Alas, I sit upon my hands and watch the sunrise over the trees and smell the destiny of loss surrounding my freezing bones.

I will not beg, or woe is I? Rather, I will await an opportunity to be planned at my time. Then the king's son, as his father before him, will dance to my tune.

Mixing Out

Mixing with the turnips, his coat of arms had bled their
cannons. It was the time of execution and bereavement.
Many men had fled their strips of land and lost many
hands. But wizards and dragons drove on to cartwheel their
enthusiasm for the cause. Waterfalls had washed away the
tears of yesterday's men and replaced them with a rabbit
warren of the new brave. Fortress walls were no more as
people had long stepped back into the surrounding fields
and countryside. The enemy had retired and had nowhere
else to be. The swallows had returned, and the blossom
showed its luck after many an empty refusal. The sun
appeared above the horizon and seemed to be warmer
now. Thus, peace had ambled into clover and made do
with repair. Even the shyness of the deer had poked forth
their heads as if ordered by nature. To close one's eyes and
breathe the air as full stop became word hops of informing
the next village gate. With peace now secured, the mudlarks
could cleanse their wares and rummage around, and there
were no more frustrations to hate.

The Journey

It was a cold and lonely walk down the lane, wrapped up against November's icy chill. His long-brimmed hat over his tunic coat kept him warm, and his breeches, combined with above-ankle-length boots, portrayed a man of some comfort. Grey hair and hazel eyes possibly indicated he was in his late middle years. His shoulder bag contained his life belongings. Yet he had no horse and was walking so promptly, for he had a mile of many or more to safely go, to protect him from any fears. The lane fields either side had mighty oaks to keep him company, as did the occasional swig of wine. He did breathe in the air and knew that for now all was calm and new. He was heading to advance his day, as the torments of angst had ravaged his previous soul-defying play, with their skyward broomsticks and jesting jousts of "A ring a ring of roses," that well-known rhyme of pain and endgame fall. For his village yonder had all believed their happiness to be sneezing and sleeps embracing call. To skyward clear he had walked with head held high and not crossed a soul as single as he. Only the occasional horse-riding clergy, who begged him to go away and flee. The frost had absconded the ground and dallied in the air to chill his bones to grasp its hooks and claws to squeeze the breath from no more lungs to fit. Yet he believed in his next village yonder, where all would hopefully sit. Not in death mask rows, but ably to duty and perform, as he was a practising herbal gent of repute and known for his honest deeds display, and safety must surely arrive at its destination soon, or all would be lost.

Castles And Kings

Living behind the splendour of castles and kings. Dreaming
in your head as the fool hardly sings. Walking the
battlements with deranged thoughts about foes. What did
the merchants pay for your arrogance and clothes? Suits
of armour with their empty souls. Soldiers in battle dress
slaughtered in abandoned holes. Yet furnishings and loot
and hostages you kept. Moats were all protected with water,
which meandered and slept. Breach up the drawbridge
as time will tick on and consecrate your fractured land.
Beyond your parlour tricks will descend a monster's hand.
To steal your mirrored vanity and exploit your empire,
sleep. Better declare peace soon, or see through walls that
will fracture to speckled glass, as eyesight blindly weeps.

Nature's Kiss

Slowly she arose from her bed. What is this the angel said?
Such music in my head.It reminds me of the swaying
blossom in the breeze, and what that brings, joy and loft,
like lambs so agile and soft. For now I breathe you flowers,
as sweet as wine to drink, as she let her soul sink within the
lush lawn of day, to close her eyes and watch memories
ably pray, like moving images flicker into life, as birds witter
and loop and stray all good on this sun bleached May.
Never gaze low, but look up to the mountains height and to
view the clouds trying to dance in white, avoiding fools and
distant wails of days not like this.

The Lamb

What are you that bleats in the day and sometimes at
night, standing with your flock all clothed in wool? I see
you trying to hide together as one with your stance radiant
like the sun. You are the lamb in the field of freedom,look
with your gaze if you must on me said she,now turning
to view the gate. Walk if you must into the next part of
life with that emblem of choice on your coat, you belong
to the fields of chance to quote "soul stained forever" but
with clarity to see. We shall listen intensely, and perchance
maybe to be. Do air-lined lungs give you that sound—
spiritual, wandering, alive, and so loud? For the eyes of the
flock command, knowing and aware, saying beware our
togetherness, for we are the Lamb and we shall hold you to
account if you misbehave, so save us from our fate, and let
us go asunder to quietly walk around, to explore, to greet,
and with our bodies amicably seek, maybe to seek a cheer
on this lively hilly ground.

Summer Ghost

It materialises in shimmering air, transient shadow, in its own maze, silent whispers trailing. Its ethereal essence becomes entwined, with laughter, blossoms, and sweet lemonade. Spectral harmony, neither seen nor defined, yet palpable, like memories gently viewed. And as the sun sinks, painting skies ablaze, This summer ghost emerges from the deep, waltzing through fireflies' ephemeral haze, phantom ballad, secrets safely sheathed. Its footsteps tread the dewy morning's cusp. In fields of thistles, where time takes its toll, a solitary wanderer, yearning to adjust, To the living world and its impassioned plea. But when the moon ascends on the starlit stage, The summer ghost grows weary, fading away. Enveloped in darkness, where memories engage, In an eternal dance, neither here nor there.

Before I Die

I want to dream as a child, performing playground tricks and chasing puppy dog tails. Touching the clouds and kissing the full moon, with my lips, to dance with angel dust, as a rainbow shines my clocks, and soul rests my bones to keep till dawn's waking light.

Chips

I will eat chips tonight and dance in my cotton socks, watching brushes paint my mirrors as music swamps my ears. Content, as I smell the dew from morning's kiss, lifts my spirits, as Robin's peer, and dovetails with my thoughts, as they had at birth. The loneliness of the silence was as proud as my dreams could imagine. Yay. I bet the bells are ringing, and my ancestors are singing, as they raise a glass or two on this wonderful day.

Window

And the snow blew through the window slats as little mice
chewed their options. Blinkered lights searched, staring
at the haze of the moon. A child, in its wisdom, peeped
through the clouds as winter iced her covers upon the land,
reckoning for the start of the season's run.

Whispering

Fingers caressed wavy hair, their scarlet ribbons flowing in the wind. Ripples of applause from beneath silken gowns, as flesh and bone, previously cold as marble, awoke into life, unshackled from the doubt of yesteryear, drinking season's spring, and breathing into lungs air as blessed as any romantic beginning.

Fading Bulbs

What was that within my eyes? Was my mind telling me
lies? Tiny lamps with fading bulbs show images of speckled
faces. Why the black and white of frightened places? Who
is that who stares into the void? The mirror, the reflections,
the noise, as the band played hope and glory near the
sunrise, as whispers in the ears, told of charging nights,
to seek the lamps of shining lament. Was there torment,
to pay the rent of a mind so baffled in disrepair? I am a
clown within my dream, telling myself that fairy stories
have cut loose their fuse with sparkles, which damaged the
brightness of her muse. Stumbling around my hole and my
lair as the shadows embrace and hold. Merging with soot
within my cloak as my outlook rains bitter and cold.

Waking Slumber

Sunshine shone on this day, its waking slumber spreading far and wide as ships' logs remembered their orders, drifting their romances to far-off lands devoid of horizons. Maps oozed with impatience and showed their etchings for Captains to aim in all directions of the compass, with watering mouths salivating at the destination of sand castles to plunder. Greed spread its wings as bugle lips sounded the leaping waves lament, with hopeful hearts leading sailors to skip their duties and toil in sewing cloth to wrap their impending booties.

Seven Moons

Seven moons prayed for seven dreams as they rose beyond sunset to take another peek. Above the horizon, seven kisses awaited their turn to flaunt blossom lips. Chatterboxes talked seven times before walking their paths to homeward gates. Sips from creatives mixed their seven rainbows to flaunt their ideas on canvas. Seven singers sang seven songs for love to be reborn. And all the while, seven poems performed on seven stages for seven pages of memories.

Spirits All Moan

For you sit staring as a child with a tiny balloon. Smiling at the sky beneath a pale rising moon. Doubling down on your frosty thoughts of spinning games and lemon sherbet of memories past. Thoughts of the atmosphere with others in the cast. Dipping pink gin and listening to her playing the mandolin, with bread crumbs slipping through sticky fingers, as bottle top booze lost her shoes and a grumbling Santa gets the sack. Rooftop antics are quiet this year, as a mumbling prayer has lost her knack. Even the stars steal a crime, downing champagne with a guzzle of wine. The end of the dream as swollen eyes glance at home. No one there, of course, as the spirits all moan.

Orbs Of The Passing Wind

I should have composed music for our ears and painted scenery for our eyes. We should have danced all night upon the mountaintops, watching the wavy lights and streamers glow as dawn's advancing day. We could have cherry-picked our sonnets and read poems till dry mouths bit dusk. Floating past swan and duck as water falls gently, with boatmen paring their strokes of gentle rhythm. All the while, we kissed and hugged in our dream. For we are orbs of the passing wind, begging for the simplicity of redemption.

Winters Song

Twas the night before the frost when all and sundry became lost. With snowflakes falling onto frozen mud-splattered ground. There was no sound from nature's emptiness call. For all the sensible ones were absent and safe within their halls and walls. It was a full moon that shone with its beams to encourage fools to flee and go. Yet an owl in a tree yonder by nearby wood hooted her call to mate in the distance to home, if you please. As human fish upon the ground did dally, and some possibly froze. As ponds and rivers unswept or crept to nowhere as their icicle tags bloomed to flowing cease. It was the winter's ever-present yearly crease that captured the mood without any squabble or delay. Even livestock outside a barn in a field bleat their masters' grief. Only the thief Jack lingers upon their back and slippery make their track to homeward trek. It is the howling wind perhaps that ambles upon the lackey and causes unease. Even the breath of outdoor warriors upon a late walk or ramble to photograph or film this amble. Slowly and desperately, they hope to find their home or cottage, warm their clothes by ample chairs, and sit near a log fire to compliment their weary bones as they close their eyes and relax. Thoughts of angst perhaps when sounds roamed in earshot and would surround their foe to tremble, gate, and ill. Yet that was memories ago, and only the silence bitten with skill would make a similar whine as it ceased due to the coldness and bitterness of the way. For this was the coming of winter's song, and for weeks she would orchestrate her play to stay and sway.

Wandering

Hiding in the shadows. Battening down the hatches, quietly performing magic with thoughts upon the run. Staring at the star struck and laughing. Doing simple cart wheels with sayers above. Writing in the parchments to formulate good health. Clocking all the time restraints and winding back the days. Looking through the telescope to see into the maze. Eternal wandering spirit whose soul is in the sky.

The Skeleton Dance

Choking upon a crusty loaf bones grin at the scene surrounding his haste. For grabbing a partner from the cemetery below showed he had good taste. Looking his Sunday best as he played the xylophone upon his rusty old chest. Maybe to impress the ladies and ask for a simple request. He often would dance till bone creaked against bone as ankles floundered due to age. Yet Skeleton Shoe Shine Shuffle was all the latest rage. Over enthusiasm and heads would definitely roll. Often flying through the air and landing in a hole. A waist-held clench was a bone-rising affair, as it certainly took courage to get to grips with holding on till dawn. But mostly it ended in bits as hands shot lost and legs went AWOL as the whole dance went crackers and forlorn.Yet on they went with rib-tickling merriment as skeletons danced the waltz. No need to rewrite certificates, however, as no one betrayed a pulse. It was, however, all good fun as bones rattled eerily into the moonlit night. Before, of course, they vanished quickly near morning's approaching light.

The Slave

Why do you not let me go free? Away into the night and
mercy's flight. These chains around my ankles and wrists
will not hold me for long. For I will imprint my birth right
within your bones to shake you to oblivion. I will not sit in
stench within the bowels of this ship with a hundred more.
Swaying and lagging to the rocking of rotting timbers and
that smell of destitute agony and death. Listening to the
moans of flies being eaten as food is so scarce that even
the crew ration themselves to fever. For upon deck our
torn sails from the tempests anger has ravished the cloth
to swing violently to starboard drifting us ever closer to
Dante's kingdom, perhaps where, in league with Neptune,
we will plummet to the ocean's floor and never more to
squeeze out a breath. My rags are hiding sores on my
dry skin as my tongue has swollen to such a height that
coughing might encourage a fit. My eyes bulge as though
sad and I see only hazy glimpses of things twittering into
languages foreign and now unknown to me. My head about
to explode implores my brains to boil away and so end this
desperate flirtation with this below decks shithole nonsense.

Plea

And as the sun rises, painting skies ablaze.
This summer ghost emerges from the deep.
Waltzing through fireflies' ephemeral haze.
phantom ballad.
Secrets safely sheathed.
Its footsteps tread the dewy morning's cusp.
In fields of thistles where time takes its toll.
A solitary wanderer yearning to adjust,
To the living world,
With its impassioned plea.

Supper's Ready

For I am at day's end entering sleep.

Even without a blink,

I can hear the sound of sheep.

Washed over by morning rain in the hills.

As humans leg it in all directions,

Hedging their bets with Father Time.

And to see the moon's horizon,

Showing up near twilight's withering.

To arise triumphantly,

With Starlight's opulent band.

Watching flower petals close,

And shut up shop.

As silence plagues the will.

Now supper's ready.

With evensong having her fill.

Stardust

When I die,
I hope someone will hold my hand.
Lifting me up above the sinking sand.
With tears of memories floating my boat.
As I remember past years.
Within an oasis of fellow travellers.
Praying that my subscription to life,
Is framed for posterity.
For I was a blank canvas,
painting into the night.

Ramble

Alone with my thoughts and brambles. To seek the daylight. Let me do the things I may ask. May my thesis enlighten my task. Make me have wisdom on my journey. Keep me strong.

When stars shine in the heavens, make me humble in prayer. Maybe this calling came from spirit,to see through the eyes of a child. Let me have wisdom to succeed.Always to be clear, learnt, and taught. Wandering with aspirations and focus, to read the clues, as an agnostic, to formulate a plan.

Empty Halls

The spirits linger, lost and all alone. Their haunting whispers hum a mournful shriek. Days long past, now faded. Each corridor, a silent, winding maze, echoes the secrets of forgotten notes, where shadows dance and flicker. Time dissolves. Ghosts of yesteryear still wander free. Memories trapped within walls vast. Restless souls, softly haunting us to death.

Not Going To Plan
(Alternative version)

Things were not going to plan.
There was a hole in the roof.
It had been there when the house was built, yet it hovered
    unconcerned and shy.
Only letting sunlight through at twilight.
It washed only when it rained.
It screamed at midnight.
Chilling when winter's wind blew through.
Sometimes it would sing.
Sometimes it would play the piano.
But mostly it was a hole.
Peering into darkness and plotting games.

Shallow Grave

A shallow grave has been dug,
below the moon's gaze.
Where secrets whispered.
Silent comfort of the departed.
Ashen clouds, weathered and worn,
bowed in reverence.
Footprints erased.
No trace remained.
Hallowed ground tinged with lonely woe.
Here lies a soul.
Eternally unknown.
No flowers beckoned, no mourners cried.
Only shadows cloaked in morose goodbye.
Time's ancient hands.
Cruel with every stroke.
Melodies swallowed by lingering ghosts.
Bound in eternity.

Replace The Carpets

(Alternative version)

Two stones marked the sunrise.
Awakening the light from the horizon.
As moonlight bids goodnight.
For as it did so,
little ships sailed away.
After yesterday's rampage upon the clifftops,
with a waterfall flooding her dreams.
Mrs. Stirling-Effort expressed dismay.
"I shall have to replace all the carpets"

Tie A Red Balloon To It

(Alternative version)

There was a hole in the boat.
Where only the curious did dwell.
With weary memories.
For as the visions embraced this clip,
panic rose with every water's sip.
Neptune's claws tried to play rock and roll,
blowing winter into nature's lungs.
As a typhoon sculptured the air,
whistling her tune.
For the lamps of disaster had been lit.
With only angels in their nightgowns,
praying devilishly.
Tie a red balloon to it.

The Last Poem

Coiled 'round the hearts it hoards in fire-forged chains, the chords of life's symphony gently rise and express their magic. Thus the stage was set for the encore of eternity.

Milton Keynes UK
Ingram Content Group UK Ltd.
UKHW052232051224
452013UK00004B/41